YOUR KNOWLEDGE HAS VALUE

The role and work of Mary May Simon in the reconciliation between Inuit Indigenous Peoples and the Government of Canada

Céline Rodrigues

Bibliographic information published by the German National Library:

The German National Library lists this publication in the National Bibliography; detailed bibliographic data are available on the Internet at http://dnb.dnb.de.

ISBN: 9783346657404
This book is also available as an ebook.

© GRIN Publishing GmbH
Trappentreustraße 1
80339 München

Print and binding: Books on Demand GmbH Norderstedt, Germany
Printed on acid-free paper from responsible sources.

The present work has been carefully prepared. Nevertheless, authors and publishers do not incur liability for the correctness of information, notes, links and advice as well as any printing errors.

GRIN web shop: https://www.grin.com/document/1246360

THE ROLE AND WORK OF MARY MAY SIMON IN THE RECONCILIATION BETWEEN INUIT INDIGENOUS PEOPLES AND THE GOVERNMENT OF CANADA

CÉLINE RODRIGUES
UNIVERSIDADE PORTUCALENSE

RESUMO

A líder Inuit Mary May Simon tem conseguido, através do seu longo e consistente trabalho em diferentes posições, criar uma relação saudável entre Aborígenes e o governo do Canadá no processo de justiça de transição. A aceitação do passado e das diferentes culturas e línguas, que fazem parte do vasto país que é o Canadá, revelando-se útil e importante no processo de cura. Tendo como suporte os artigos escritos por Mary Simon e discursos, estabelecer-se-á uma relação entre o seu trabalho e a reconciliação que tem sido acelerada desde 2015 no Canadá.

PALAVRAS-CHAVE: ÁRTICO, INUIT, JUSTIÇA DE TRANSIÇÃO, LEADER, MARY SIMON, RECONCILIAÇÃO

ABSTRACT

Inuit leader Mary May Simon has been able to do a long and consistence work in different positions that allow the good and healthy relationship between indigenous peoples and the government of Canada in a process of truth and reconciliation. The acceptance of the past and of the different cultures and languages that are part of a vast and diverse country such as Canada are helpful and of importance in the healing process. Through Mary Simon's articles and speeches it is possible to establish a relationship between her work and reconciliation that has been accelerating since 2015 in Canada.

KEYWORDS: ARCTIC, INUIT, LEADER, MARY SIMON, TRANSITIONAL JUSTICE, TRUTH AND RECONCILIATION

TABLE OF CONTENTS

INTRODUCTION

The constitutional monarchy of Canada has been working, during the first quarter of this century, in healing with the past. A process included in what is known as transitional justice in order to repair the atrocities of the colonialism period and even events occurred in the 20th century, as it is the case in Canada, with the Residential Schools.

It is important to remind that before Europeans arrived in Canada and "discovered" the Arctic region, First Nations, Inuit and Métis were already there. Those first inhabitants have lost their sovereignty, in some cases their language and culture along the way, due to forced assimilation. To note that indigenous people are 10 % in a total population of 4 million people in the Arctic (Koivurova, Tervo and Stiepen, 2008, p.3).

Repairing the past does not mean erasing what has been done at some historic moment. Human beings can easily attack the ones that they see as different. Human evolution tries to repair, by learning from past mistakes, and understand that all win if they are all able to accept each other´s differences. That is what Roald Amundsen did. What helped him and his crew to pass through the Northwest Passage in 1906 was learning from those - Inuit - who are in contact with nature, know and understand how the ecosystem functions in order to survive. It was key to success.

This knowledge and wisdom are now being accepted in Canadian society. Since the second half the 20th century, and until the moment these words are being written, the recognition of Inuit as first inhabitants, through modern treaties giving them back their land, self-government, apologising for what has been done unfairly and reconciliating within the same territory, is being effective.

All this has been witnessed by an Inuit woman leader known by the name of Mary May Simon.

In this paper, the goal is to explain the contribution of Mary May Simon, through her work in different places throughout the last four decades, which allows to establish the connection between the truth and reconciliation process going on in Canada and her visible labour, in three parts:

> 1)- the biography of Mary May Simon is presented, showing its consistency and resilience as Inuit leader in different positions and places;
>
> 2)- the intention in this part is to focus on the importance of the presence of Mary Simon in two moments – Inuit Circumpolar Council and Arctic Council –

where there is a crucial role of Inuit Indigenous Peoples in participating within the international community and about their recognition at different levels: national, regional and international;

3)- the office she is at now since July 2021 can be seen as the supra recognition of her work and the confirmation of the shift of Canada in what concerns the will of a healthy relationship between Indigenous Peoples and the Government of Canada.

This way, it can be concluded that being Inuit and Canadian means to have a complementary identity that this Inuit woman leader personifies. Nevertheless, it applies to all indigenous peoples.

The methodology used for this work is qualitative, mainly based on articles written by Mary May Simon, communications/conferences and speeches of Mary May Simon. Through her words, written or spoken, the fight, the pride, the resilience, the will to protect, help and empower Indigenous Peoples are felt. It is also interesting to notice the vision of this diplomat in her writings that seemed to have been interpreted like recommendations in this country that seems to, still, be discovering its territory and people: the Arctic is also Canada and indigenous people are also Canadian.

Shall the South assimilate the North, so they become one.

1- KNOWING MARY MAY SIMON

Inuit are patient and practical people.
(Simon, 2011, p.888)

Mary Jeannie May Simon or Ningiukudluk (meaning "bossy little old lady"[1]) was born in 21 august 1947 in Kangirsualujjuaq, Nunavik, Québec. Daughter of Inuk mother and English Canadian Southern father who worked at the local Hudson´s Bay Company post. Simon grew up in the Inuit community having access to their traditional lifestyle, camping, hunting among other activities as she describes in a conference in 2000. She had a formal education and was also home schooled under her father´s tutelage and got her graduation by correspondence courses. While growing, Simon is becoming aware of the differences between "white people" and Aboriginal people (Simon, 2000). The consciousness of this difference and witnessing the militarization of the Arctic pushed her to write a letter to the Canadian government explaining what was happening and asking "them to please stop the overflights" (Gaviria, 2013, p.3). This episode can be considered as the beginning of the future active and activist role of Mary May Simon. Although, she will first have an experience as producer at Canadian Broadcasting corporation´s Northern Service in the beginning of 1970´s of the 20th century.

In the conference held in 2000[2], Simon states that her first experience on Aboriginal rights issues was during the negotiations for the *James Bay and Northern Quebec Agreement* in 1975, which was the first land claim agreement in Canada. As a positive consequence of this agreement, a foundation was built, the Makivik Corporation in 1978, being Mary Simon vice president in the period 1978-1980 and president from 1983 to 1985. This foundation had the purpose to implement the agreement. With the knowledge acquired during this time in this foundation, she then joined the organization Inuit Tapirisat Kanatamai where she defended the need of a clear and legal definition in what is understood as the basic right to self-government. This would lead to negotiations known as *Charlottetown Accord*, with the goal of a referendum, but it was not successful. Nonetheless, and because Simon considered that Indigenous rights and equality lack of clarity, she participated in the elaboration of the section 35 of 1982

---

[1] Mary May Simon explained her name during her speech as Governor General. (Tunney, C., Major, D. (2021, 26 July) Mary Simon officially becomes Canada's first Inuk Governor General. *CBC News*. Available at: https://www.cbc.ca/news/politics/mary-simon-installed-as-governor-general-1.6114622)
[2] Simon, M.M. (2000). From Kangiqsualujjuaq to Copenhagen: A Personal Jouney. Northern Review, [online], dec. 2000, n. 22, [consulted 10 December 2021]. ISSN 1929-6657. Available at: https://thenorthernreview.ca/index.php/nr/article/view/320

Constitution which states that the Inuit land claims are equivalent to treaty rights. That way, protection is granted by the constitution.

Throughout the years Simon feels "that very basic human rights were not available to many of the world's indigenous peoples" (Simon, 2000).

From 1980 to 1986 she was Executive Council at the Inuit Circumpolar Conference (ICC), created in 1977 now Inuit Circumpolar Council and she served as president in the period 1986-1992 This organization, inspired by oral history tradition, was able to join Inuit indigenous peoples from around the world - Alaska, Greenland and later Siberia - realizing the dream of her grandmother of a global Inuit reunion (Curry & Raman-Wilms, 2021). This unity prioritizes the protection and safeguard of the Arctic environment as well as enhancing social and economic development.

Following the time line presented, she was appointed in 1993 Co-Director and Secretary to the Royal Commission on Aboriginal Peoples (created by the Prime Minister Brain Mulroney after the Oka Crisis) where she had the opportunity to "better understand the complex political and social issues with which Canadian Aboriginal peoples have been grappling" (Simon, 2000).

In 1994, Mary Simon was appointed Canada's Ambassador for Circumpolar Affairs until 2003 working directly with the Canadian government in developing "partnerships based on an emerging recognition of the benefits of working together in seeking solutions to common problems, be they environmental, social or political" (*idem*). She considers her main responsibility as reinvigorating the Arctic Council initiative as well as developing a foreign policy for Canada that can reflect human security. Being, at the same time, negotiator for the Arctic Council, she met with all involved in the project to pass the message of Canada in the cooperation of all Arctic states that share common issues. At that time, she felt expectations were very high because the north expected her to deliver.

During the period 2006-2012, she was the president of Inuit Tapirit Kanatami (represents around 40,000 Inuit in Northern Canada) and it was during her presidency that Prime Minister Stephen Harper's made a formal apology. This act was perceived as an "end of the dark period in the collective history as a nation" in Simon's words (2008).

Her curricula go on as Chancellor of Trent University (1995-1999), Chair at National Committee on Inuit Education (2008-2014) with the implementation of a report in 2011 entitled: *First Canadians, Canadians First: A National Strategy for Inuit Education*.

She is the founder of the Arctic Children and Youth Foundation (2012).

She also served as Minister´s Special Representative having presented a report with the title *A new shared Arctic Leadership Model* in 2017 that will help in the revision of the Arctic and Northern Framework Policy in 2019.

The office she is running at moment, since July 2021, is as Governor General, appointed by the prime Minister Justin Trudeau and accepted by the Queen Elizabeth II will allow to build the bridges still missing between both parts along with the reconciliation. Some saw the lack of French knowledge as not understandable for this nomination, but her bilingualism in Inuktitut[3] and English are positive in a becoming inclusive Canada and she has showed availability to learn French, and has prove it in her speeches since then. It is important to recall that she was born in Québec where French is an official language. Yet, because she is Inuit, learning French was not allowed to her when she was a child.

In this first part of this paper, and after an exhausting presentation of her work, it is considered to be included in what is defined as transitional justice. Colonization had negative impact in relations between North and South and Europeans´ actions still remain in falling apart different cultures that shall look at each other as complementary. It seems to be the next goal of Mary May Simon.

---

[3] The United Nations defined the Decade of Indigenous Languages (2022-2032) that prioritizes the empowerment of users of indigenous language.

2- ON THE WAY TO RECOGNITION...

Hi, I'm nobody[4]
(Simon, 2011, p.881)

*This wisdom from the North, is I believe, one of the most
important aspects of the heritage that polar regions bring
to humanity*
(Simon, 1997, p.8)

The processes of land claim agreements (modern treaties) that occurred in: 1975 (James Bay and northern Quebec Agreement); 1999 (the new territory of Nunavut); 2005 (Labrador[5]); and currently for Nunavik, are to be considered as part of the recognition of Inuit, who are undoubtedly first inhabitants of the country. Mary Simon is the confirmation that Inuit and other indigenous peoples still have their own culture, language and history.

According to Timo Koivurova (2011) the development of international law regarding indigenous peoples has been rapid since the 80´s of last century. The same author considers that the evolution of the 1989 convention to the United Nations Declaration on the Rights of Indigenous Peoples (2007) is "the mark of 20 years of negotiations between states and indigenous peoples in recognizing their right to self-determination (articles 3 and 4)" (p176). Agreeing with the author, it can be added that the resilience and determination of Mary Simon, not only in Canada but in international forums, contributed to this actual consideration and evolution.

Canada has taken seriously the question of repairing and making peace with the past. Since 2015, with the Prime Minister Justin Trudeau, changes are happening quickly.

For this second part, it was difficult to decide which moment of her service shall be framed within this context and process of healing. Nevertheless, after some reflection, and according to her writings and the progress of transitional justice in the country, it can be considered that the Inuit Circumpolar Council and the Arctic Council exemplify how Simon contributed to the recognition of Indigenous peoples that will, slowly but surely, lead to the reconciliation (part 3).

---

[4] "In his book *Who owns the Arctic*, University of Columbia law professor Michael Byers relates a telling story: "John Amagoalik, as the former president of the Inuit Tapisirat of Canada, recalls attending a meeting of the United Nations where a foreign diplomat blithely stated that "nobody lived in the Arctic". Amagoalik approached the diplomat afterwards, held out his hand and said "Hi, I'm nobody"." (Simon, M.M. (2011). Canadian Inuit: Where we have been and where we are going. *International Journal* vol. 66, No. 4, The Arctic is hot, part II, pp. 879- 891, p.881)

[5] Discovered by João Fernandes who might have reached Greenland - Terra do Lavrador - and the name migrated to south to what is now known as Labrador. For more information: Hiller, J.K. (2004) The Portuguese Explorers. *Heritage Newfoundland and Labrador*. Available at: https://www.heritage.nf.ca/articles/exploration/portuguese.php

By the end of this chapter, the "recommendation" below, written by Mary Simon in 1990 in her response to the Global Consultation on the realization of the right to development as a Human Right of the United Nations while President at the Inuit Circumpolar Council, will be confirmed:

> (...) indigenous peoples urgently require access to relevant international and national forums. Without our direct and ongoing input, it is unrealistic to assume that state governments or the international community as a whole can adequately identify our basic concerns. Nor can they unilaterally protect and advance our rights and interest (Simon, 1990, p.3)

A. INUIT CIRCUMPOLAR COUNCIL

The Inuit Circumpolar Council (ICC) was formed in 1977. It represents about 180,000 Inuit in Canada, Alaska, Greenland and Russia. The unity made sense after understanding they were facing the same common ssues: environmental, social and economic. Simon is in some way shocked at the time by how much they have in common and how much they "do not want to change their way of life, which is tied to the environment as a living resource" as we can read in the article of *Maclean's* Magazine of February 6, 1995[6].

In 1983, with Mary Simon as Executive director the ICC was recognised with Consultative Status by the United Nations, which helped to have a very active participation and role since then. Shadian, quoted by Olga Gavaria, considers that "it is more than an NGO as it provides a collective transnational identity that challenges traditional notions of sovereignty in international relations" (Shadian cited by Gavaria 2013, p.79). This consideration matches Simon's (1990) idea of how this organization has been able to insist in having indigenous peoples involved in national and international forums as there is a "profound relationship between development, human rights and peace and any policy - or decision - making concerning development in the Arctic must fully take into account all of these factors" (p.1).

It is not until 2007 that the United Nations adopted the Declaration on the Rights of Indigenous Peoples which includes "the core right of self-determination". After that, this transnational organization presented a document entitled "A circumpolar Inuit declaration on sovereignty in the Arctic" (2009) in which "indigenous peoples have the right to self-determination and where states are reminded of their obligations to indigenous peoples under a variety of international agreements" (Simon, 2011, p. 886). Canada only accepted the UN Declaration in 2016.

It can be stated that another goal achieved by the Inuit diplomat, was the inclusion as observers status of this organization in the Arctic Environmental Protection Strategy (AEPS). Later, it will be one of the six organizations that have the permanent participant status in the Artic Council with important role and impact not only in land claims but also in "drafting many reports" in what concerns pollutants and their impacts and how "global warming affects people's life" in Arctic region (Huebert, 2008, pp.12-13) being the new threat for indigenous peoples (Koivurova, Tervo and Stiepen, 2008, p.3).

---

[6] Canadian Encyclopedia (2014, 11 March). Simon first native ambassador Available at: https://www.thecanadianencyclopedia.ca/en/article/simon-first-native-ambassador#

In 2006, this organization defined the day 7 of November as the International Inuit Day in order to celebrate the Arctic and the people that live there. It coincides with the birthday of Eben Hopson Sr., an Arctic political leader and founder of the ICC.

B. ARCTIC COUNCIL

Mary May Simon participated as negotiator, being Canada´s Ambassador for Circumpolar Affairs at the same time. The will was the creation of the Arctic Council (AC), which predecessor was the Arctic Environmental Protection Strategy (AEPS) in 1991. The latter focused on protecting the environment and the idea was launched by Michael Gorbachev in 1987. The countries that joined the AEPS, by signing the Rovaniemi Declaration, were: Canada, Denmark, Finland, Iceland, Norway, Sweden, Russia and the United States of America (Koivurova, 2011, p.171; Simon, 1997).

From its very the beginning, the AEPS distinguished itself by its intention to engage Arctic indigenous peoples in the cooperation and recognition of their right to be consulted in any issues concerning their homelands. At the time three Indigenous Peoples Organizations (IPO) joined the organization with the observer status: Inuit Circumpolar Council, Saami Council and Russian Association of Indigenous Peoples of the North. As the author Rob Huebert (2008) affirms: "their insistence on including northern Aboriginal representation was both inspiring and forward thinking" (p.13).

It is relevant to refer that in 1994 was created the Indigenous Peoples Secretariat (IPS) as an entity of the AC, as mentioned in the Ottawa Declaration (1996), having its own board and budget. Its functions are to assist Permanent Participants within the Arctic Council and to promote indigenous culture, amid others. The Chair of the Governing Board is chosen by the PP and communications are held in English and Russian languages. In 2016, the Indigenous Peoples Secretariat was relocated from Copenhagen (Denmark) to Tromso (Norway).

Simon[7] travelled a lot during negotiations period for what will become the Arctic Council, conducting many meetings, mainly to obtain formal support from the United States of America, announced by Bill Clinton in 1995 (Huebert, 2008, p.12). Aligned with the growing acknowledgement of the special relationship of indigenous peoples to the Arctic region, the Arctic countries assigned the special status of Permanent

---

[7] Mary May Simon referred in an interview that if the PP´s role were diminished, Canada would walk out of the negotiations. (Brøndbo, S. (2016) Interview with Mary Simon. Shared Voices Magazine 2016 Special Issue. *UiT The Arctic University of Norway.* Available at: https://www.uarctic.org/shared-voices/shared-voices-magazine-2016-special-issue/interview-with-mary-simon/)

Participants[8] (PP) to the three IPOs in 1996. Later, the number of PP doubled to make up the present six, and the Aleut International Association (1998), the Arctic Athabaskan Council (2000) and the Gwich'in Council International (2000) were appointed Permanent Participants (Koivurova, 2011, p.173; Simon, 1997).

The Article 2 of Ottawa Declaration states that: "the number of PP should at any time be less than the number of members". Mary Simon explains in her article "Building partnerships: perspectives from the Arctic" (1997) that "Permanent Participants attend most Arctic Council meetings, but take no part in decision-making". Tough, they can influence states in their last answer, decision-making.

The author Timo Koivurova (2011) considers that "gray zones" remain regarding PP status and he questions what can happen to them if a treaty is to be established as the one in Antarctica (pp.189-190). Considering the positive change regarding the role and importance achieved in local, regional and global participation of the indigenous peoples in multi-level governance, it can be cautiously said that, any change that might occur in the future, it would be difficult (if not impossible in the present moment) to not include, at any moment or level of decision-making, representants of indigenous peoples. Still, it shall not be taken as granted. Their presence can be even more effective.

---

[8] The Arctic Council was defined in 1996 with the Ottawa Declaration in which categories of participants are defined and designated as members, permanent participants and observers (Koivurova, T. (2011). The status and role of Indigenous Peoples in Arctic International Governance. The Yearbook of Polar Law. Vol. 3, pp. 169-192. p. 173).

3- ...AND RECONCILIATION

My view is that reconciliation is a way of life[9].

(Simon, 2021)

As referred along the pages, a change is occurring in Canada with the truth and reconciliation process. In the last seven years, by the hand of the Prime Minister Justin Trudeau, an acceleration is visible in what concerns the reconciliation and the establishment of a strong relationship between Inuit and Government of Canada[10].

The Truth and Reconciliation Agreement was established in 1998 in Canada considered an individual and collective process, the first national event took place in June 2010 and concluded its mandate in 2015, with a 94 "calls to action" report as recommendations. The first anniversary of the national day happened in 30 September 2021. September 29 was the eve of this first National Day, an event where Governor General Mary Simon and Prime Minister Justin Trudeau heard the stories of the survivors of residential schools. Justin Trudeau recognized the courage of those who shared traumatic stories of a dark moment in Canada's history. That is why the healing process is not only for indigenous peoples as the prime minister said: "until we understand as a country that each one of us story is all of our stories, there can be no truth, there can be no reconciliation." (Trudeau, 2021[11]).

The process of reconciliation is a long and hard process, not only politically speaking, but also and mainly psychology speaking. It revives memories in survivors and descendants of those who heard the stories. It must be understood as an individual and collective memory. It still hurts for those who lived in the Residential Schools and / or had to be relocated, and reviving bad moments is harmful and heartbreaking. Those wounds take a lifetime to heal[12].

---

[9] Tunney, C., Major, D. (2021, 26 July) Mary Simon officially becomes Canada's first Inuk Governor General. *CBC News*. Available at: https://www.cbc.ca/news/politics/mary-simon-installed-as-governor-general-1.6114622

[10] That seems to be relevant also in a moment that there is a growing scepticism about monarchy´s role in Canada as mentioned in the article of The Guardian: Cecco. L. (2021, 6 July). 'Historic' step as Trudeau appoints Canada's first Indigenous governor general. *The Guardian*. Available at: https://www.theguardian.com/world/2021/jul/06/mary-simon-canada-first-indigenous-governor-general-trudeau

[11] Bryden, J. (2021, 29 September). Eve of 1st national day for truth and reconciliation sees May Simon, Trudeau call for unity. *The Canadian Press*. Available at: https://globalnews.ca/news/8232737/truth-reconciliation-day-mary-may-simon-trudeau/

[12] "Transitional justice – with its interrelated pillars of truth, justice, reparation and guarantees of non-recurrence – makes an essential contribution in navigating complex spaces of transition, marked by rapid change, competing interests, pain and simmering grievances, and where narratives and memories are at risk of extreme polarization and instrumentalization. Transitional justice processes, when they are context-specific, nationally-owned and focused on the needs of victims, can connect, empower and transform societies. Through dialogue and confrontation of ideas and experiences, transitional justice seeks to make connections between victims and perpetrators, political factions, communities, and across generations." (UN Office of the High Commissioner for Human Rights, Thematic Paper: Peacebuilding, Sustaining Peace and Transitional Justice, 2020, p.2)

In this last part of the paper, it is considered that the culmination of reconciliation materializes with Mary Simon's nomination as Governor General of Canada last July 2021. It is not the first time that Mary May Simon is presented to be assigned Governor General. It occurred in 2010, but the findings of dead children in Residential Schools changed the course of history back then. It does not mean that her work stopped as presented in the first chapter.

It seems Mary Simon is the right person at the right moment in this office (a non-partisan and political office), as the Arctic is becoming more competitive and making peace with the past is relevant and important to both parts. Past can not be changed but all can learn from it and become better persons, individually and collectively, by accepting each other and learning from each other.

What does it mean to be Governor General of Canada? In the official website[13] of the Governor General of Canada it is possible to read the following definition:

> The governor general's responsibilities include carrying out constitutional duties, serving as commander-in-chief, representing Canada at home and abroad, encouraging excellence and bringing Canadians together. (Duties of Governor General of Canada, 2021)

This description suits very well Mary Simon, considering also that "the Governor General is also in the unique position to foster mutual understanding and reconciliation between Indigenous and non-Indigenous peoples"[14]. In order to "deepen people-to-people ties and strengthen Canada's relationships with international partners"[15], Simon included indigenous peoples in her team to her first visit to Germany last October 2021: poet laureate, writer Louise Bernice Halfe (known by the Cree name Sky Dancer), Lisa Koperqualuk (the vice-president of international affairs for Inuit Circumpolar Council Canada). Last visit by a Governor General to Germany occurred in 2001.

Her will and determination to contribute positively to this change that will allow a peaceful reconciliation within Canada's society, made her promised, in her speech at the parliamentary session on November 2021, the construction of a national monument to survivors of residential schools[16].

---

[13] Governor General of Canada. Constitutional Duties Available at: https://www.gg.ca/en/governor-general/role/responsibilities/constitutional-duties
[14] Idem
[15] Idem
[16] Pelletier, J. (2021, 24 November,) Canada's Liberal party promises to cut child care costs in the North. *Nunatsiaq News*. Available at: https://www.arctictoday.com/canadas-liberal-party-promises-to-cut-child-care-costs-in-the-north/

This woman is certainly a promoter of reconciliation. The process does not end with her nomination but it is a step forward to a peaceful healing process in Canada (not only with Inuit but with all indigenous peoples).

CONCLUSION

"Bossy little old lady", woman, Inuit, leader, ambassador, diplomat, president, builder of bridges, visionary, resilient, respectful, communicative, peaceful. Many are the words to try to define or describe Mary May Simon. While reading her writings it feels like she always has transmitted a message of cooperation. Her words in paper are transformed into concrete actions. Those first inhabitants had and still have a lot to teach to those who are not able to live in those icy places. The past is not in her writings, nevertheless, and due to her new position, it has been more recurrent to hear her about the past, her story and the importance of reconciliation. She helps the reader to look ahead and her visionary thinking is easily interpreted as recommendations, nationally, regionally and internationally. She cherishes her background, traditions and values and expects future generations to keep that respect over those traditions and values. "Being a leader means being a person of honesty, integrity and determination, on good days and bad," she told her audience in 2012[17]. She is indeed an example of a leader who has learnt to accept and live with her two identities (north and south) whether using one or another in different circumstances. That is why the two identities (and cultures) are complementary. And this is how Canadians and Inuit (Indigenous and *qublunaaq* - non-indigenous) should look at her and themselves at this moment.

It is hoped this paper can contribute in academic research about the Arctic region and the different topics yet to be studied in International Relations about this "wild" region, internationally, regionally and domestically.

A question is left here for further research works: what about British Crown (even France, or Portugal) in this truth and reconciliation process[18]?

There is still work to do, and in the words of the Queen Elizabeth II in her message to mark Canada's first National Day of Truth and Reconciliation:

> I join with all Canadians on this first National Day for Truth and Reconciliation
>
> to reflect on the painful history that Indigenous peoples endured in residential

---

[17] Betkowski, E. (2012, 18 June). Canada's Arctic ambassador urges cross-boundary thinking. University of Alberta. Available at: https://www.uarctic.org/news/2012/6/canada-s-arctic-ambassador-urges-cross-boundary-thinking/
[18] The Vancouver Sun. Really Harper, Canada has no history of colonialism? *The Vancouver Sun*. (27, September 2009). Considering the statement of the Prime Minister Stephen Harper in 2009 in a G20 meeting: "We also have no history of colonialism...". Available at: https://vancouversun.com/news/community-blogs/really-harper-canada-has-no-history-of-colonialism

schools in Canada, and on the work that remains to heal and to continue to

build an inclusive society. (Queen Elizabeth II, 2021[19])

Mary May Simon represents the new image of Canada at local, regional and global levels. The Arctic and its peoples are heritage of humanity.

---

[19] Royal UK. (2021, 30 September). The Queen's message to mark Canada´s first National Day of Truth and Reconciliation. Available at: https://www.royal.uk/queens-message-mark-canadas-first-national-day-truth-and-reconciliation

REFERENCES

Betkowski, B. (2012, 18 June). Canada's Arctic ambassador urges cross-boundary thinking. *University of Alberta*. Available at: https://www.uarctic.org/news/2012/6/canada-s-arctic-ambassador-urges-cross-boundary-thinking/

Brøndbo, S. (2016). Interview with Mary Simon. Shared Voices Magazine 2016 Special Issue. *UiT The Arctic University of Norway*. Available at: https://www.uarctic.org/shared-voices/shared-voices-magazine-2016-special-issue/interview-with-mary-simon/

Curry, B. & Raman-Wilms, M. (2021, 6 July). Governor-General Mary Simon dedicated her career to reshaping indigenous policy in Canada. *The globe and mail*. Available at: https://www.theglobeandmail.com/politics/article-governor-general-mary-simon-dedicated-her-career-to-reshaping/

Gaviria, O. P. Inuit self-determination and postsecondary education: The case of Nunavut and Greenland. [online]. Doctoral Thesis, University of Toronto, 2013 [consulted 10 December 2021]. Available in Repositorium: https://tspace.library.utoronto.ca/bitstream/1807/65562/3/Gaviria_Olga_P_201311_PhD_thesis.pdf

Huebert, R (2008). Canada and the Changing International Arctic: At the Crossroads of Cooperation and Conflict, *Institute for Research on Public policy*. pp. 1-28. Available at: http://irpp.org/wp-content/uploads/2008/09/huebert.pdf

Koivurova, T. (2011). The status and role of Indigenous Peoples in *Arctic International Governance*. The Yearbook of Polar Law. Vol. 3, pp. 169-192. Available at SSRN: https://ssrn.com/abstract=2429175

Koivurova, T., Tervo, H., & Stępień, A. (2008). *Indigenous Peoples in the Arctic: background paper*. (pp. 1-33). *Arctic Transform*. Available at: https://www.arctic-transform.eu/download/IndigPeoBP.pdf

Simon, M.M. (1985) The Role of Inuit in International Affairs, *Études/Inuit/Studies* Vol. 9, No. 2, Politiques arctiques / Arctic policy (1985), pp. 33-38. Université Laval Available at: https://www.jstor.org/stable/42869520

Simon, M.M. (1990). Indigenous peoples and the right to development: an Inuit perspective: document / submitted by Mary Simon, Inuit Circumpolar, Inuit Circumpolar Conference. *United Nations*. Available at: https://digitallibrary.un.org/record/634037

Simon, M.M. (1997). Building partnerships: perspectives from the arctic._Behind the headlines; Toronto , vol. 54, ed. 3: 10. Available at: https://www.proquest.com/scholarly-journals/building-partnerships-perspectives-arctic/docview/204577796/se-2

Simon, M.M. (2000). From Kangiqsualujjuaq to Copenhagen: A Personal Jouney. *Northern Review*, [online], dec. 2000, n. 22, [consulted 10 December 2021]. ISSN 1929-6657. Available at: https://thenorthernreview.ca/index.php/nr/article/view/320

Simon, M.M. (2011). Canadian Inuit: Where we have been and where we are going. *International Journal* Vol. 66, No. 4, The Arctic is hot, part II, pp. 879- 891 : Sage Publications, Ltd. on behalf of the Canadian International Council. Available at: https://www.jstor.org/stable/23104399

YOUR KNOWLEDGE HAS VALUE